BLACK

WITCH

WANTING

Authored By: Keamba

For Panther,

My brilliant daughter and witch in training. Always remember that everything you will ever need you already possess within yourself.

Keamba is a poet, a mother, and the author
of Black Witch Wanting. Keamba formally
studied and received her undergraduate degree in
Philosophy with a focus in metaphysics, ethics,
and non-Western philosophical traditions. Her
book of poems Black Witch Wanting is a
culmination of her experiences as a Black woman,
a mother, and practitioner of African spiritualism
and all sorts of magic. She is also an activist that
is invested in understanding and dismantling
systems of oppression through both corporeal
and incorporeal means. She grew up and still
lives in Baltimore, MD. She loves science fiction,
reading, traveling, and spending time with her
family.

Witch

A witch,

Not insane,

An Angel forced to live a Lifetime on the mortal plane.

Trying not to let the mortal sins rub off on me.

Weighing down my heart and wings,

my heart chamber decompressing.

Too many armor breaches and my shields running at half capacity.

Feeling most of the impact from every attack and surrounded by the enemy.

Death will be a gift to me.

A gift I try not to await impatiently on my hard days and not to hasten on my worse days.

Taught

In Infinite Space, we are contained in such a small place.

Dragged down and put into strict limits,

Taught to be stupid and civic.

Dragging out lessons of basic spells and numeration,

Only to distract you from the magic of it.

Taught to be mortal and stagnant,

Talking you into globes and circles that do not quite make sense.

Theorems and Postulates that need to be cut down by Occam's razor.

Taught to be godless and crazy.

Believing a man that looks like my oppressor is God and is coming to save me,

The result of a virgin having a baby.

Taught to be slaves and complacent.

Take the King's land and dethrone his queen as the object of beauty,

And instigate a munity where there once was harmony.

Taught to be enemies of our own liberation,

Uncover our history and take back the plantation.

Burn it all down to the foundation.

To forget what you were taught is the true path to salvation.

Stars

Give hope to all the miscreants that magic does
exist

Outside the matrix, in alternate dimensions.

Like Pynchon's men tracking lovers and bombs
with stars

Agencies propagating creative expressions of stars

As people wish to become them

Gods that want to be Stars

Don't know what will become of them

Hurling through time stationary in space trying to
find an imaginary way out.

Identity

A mother and a lover

A goddess and a mistress

Liberated and a slave

A slave to my own and others mental constructs

Trying to break free

Learning the knowledge and Love of Me

I love myself unequivocally

To request revision or alteration is a violation

You were not the artist that created me

Your addition or subtracting is unnecessary

I was made in balance with all things from the beginning

Better than Picasso or even Da Vinci

My design is supreme my womb live giving and with no water my vagina is a stream.

My hair antennas like lightning rods feeding me energy from my surroundings

I encompass all and need only to be free

Love Free

Self-love complete I seek to love that which is
outside of me

Altruistic with my body

My love is free

There is no fee or rites of passage to gain entry

To my Kingdom, my temple, my sanctuary, my
yoni

I am not giving it out like candy because candy
rots teeth,

I am giving it out like the blessings and abundance
the Universe has always given me

It is not up for sale, trade, or barter, or in exchange
for a ring,

It is not a thing of enterprise but a tool of healing, a
tool of melding together lives,

Allies are made between these thighs, nothing
makes friends like love without conditions, without
apprehension, or hidden intentions

Having shared in a spiritual exchange in a sacred
dimension, we become extensions of

each other, we carry the other forever, and when
nurtured it grows roots and through

them love and knowledge is interchanged

No shame resides in my giving of sexuality that is
the sensual manifestation of my spirituality,

Like the ocean, like the streams, like the trees, my
love flows infinitely, like water,

Like oxygen it resides in abundance all around me

Ready and willing to sustain me

Divorced from society and economies

The All that is has been before and will be after
these man-made things

These disjunctive conjuring's that build mental
barriers to Unity

My free love is my protest and my ministry

Unaccursed

Damn it was epic
I was hoping it wouldn't be epic
Energy between us too kinetic
Beyond containment
Causing time and spatial displacement
A participation in the Aesthetic
My desires becoming prophetic
Just like I manifested it
Not knowing if it is to my benefit
Or my detriment. Constantly trying to get ahead of
it.
Regulate it but I end up savoring it
Trying to find ways to maintain it but
Always questioning
Could it be magic?
Never felt such an overwhelming attraction
Continually pulling me back in
Growing in on itself
Evolving into something else
Raw and Glowing
I hope this is harmless
I hope I survive this
For better or worse
I plead with the Universe
Let this beautiful love remain
Unaccursed

Magic Meeting

Born magical in a world that had long turned its back
on it
We could never quite relate to what was going on
Too innocent for the world we were born into, we
retreated into ourselves
Into our own minds where worlds have been created
and destroyed
Where we have lived out thousands of lives and
possibilities
Only leading us further into the magical realm that we
were always just that much closer too than anyone we
had ever known
Lone wolves, deviant in our paths
Secure on our thrones, minds beyond the need of
validation our peers fell slave to
Too busy trying to heal ourselves from all the pain that
we been through
I can feel that sorrow in you that same pain that
permeates me and drives me to love you, our only
sanctuary
Sometimes we meet there together, embrace to try to
stay there as long as the universe will let us, trying to
pause the world moving too fast around us

(Interlude)

Slave ships designed like the
parts in the baby's hair,

Strands of hair interlocking
like how they stacked us.

The Beast

What would happen if I brought out my beast?

That third face, the real, the things in the cavernous place

Deep down where the light can't touch.

The shit I play dumb about when the play is on and the play is off

Walking about picking up broken truths and half lies, throwing them in and watching them sink like they all do

Down to the beast

And she eats it, all the shit and she is angry

She is so angry; I keep her there in her abyss, but she is everything

Everything I want to be but am not, she is there, and she is waiting

But I fear she will replace me, though she is a more accurate reflection of my manifestations

but she is not in keeping with so many of my declarations which fall like traps around her every time she swims near the surface or looks up through the water.

Would I cease to be with her first breath of air, if she ever got out of that gray matter?

Cloth and Cotton

As she turned over onto her side she waited to feel that rush of relief that comes when she gets settled into her favorite sleeping position

Facing her left, with her left leg bent more extensively than the other in a partial fetal position

Seeking comfort and warmth in the couch pillows, finding a place where her curves are snuggled by the mixture of cloth and cotton

A comfort that for most of her life was provided by the warm body next to her

A complementary body, another god encased in flesh

Flesh so vibrant with life and warmth, the embrace so intoxicating

The back of her body pressed firmly against the front of the other

Back to chest, butt to pelvis, legs to legs

Two beings born apart, synchronized for however brief the moment

Those first few breaths after the melding, pure ecstasy, and relief

Trying not to move to break the connection, trying to soak it all in

Knowing in the back of her mind that it won't last forever

Having had high hopes on too many occasions putting too many eggs in an imperfect and fleshy basket

All her hopes and her dreams one by one loaded onto their shoulders, reassured by his embrace

The archetypal man

Strong and caring, hopefully engorged when she pushes her butt towards his pelvis

One after the other, love brings them to embrace as life and entropy tear at the strands of their tapestry little by little the bonds between threads grow weaker and more frayed

Then the body behind her turns cooler, the warmth harder to find, the connection less cohesive, and so much stuff between them

That is always the beginning of the end, after that he will leave, or she will

Again seeking comfort made of more than cloth and cotton

Human Baskets

It is not that I think this is small but no need to make it bigger

No need to make it too large to fit in its previous space too heavy
for our last cart to carry its weight

It will be harder on us now to see a smile as just a smile or
disregard an offhand remark

As I clumsily tread through my existence, you appear not like
the others by my wayside offering baskets to relieve my load

You are right in front of me

Impeding my way, I was content to juggle my eggs from hip to
hip and I had a few stashed securely between my breasts

When my load is too much to bear I am wise enough to stop and
rest and my best has been enough

Maybe I could put a few eggs on your basket and keep a few for
me, a few for later, a few for the uncertainty

But you will not agree, you want all my eggs from me all so
dangerously corralled in one flawed basket

Do I need a basket?

How long can I juggle cargo so precious?

The whole of my hopes and dreams

Relinquished for one

That I will not again have to carry them alone

Every love story is a tragedy if you

Wait long enough

TaP

Our lives collide, more like coalesced over troubled lives

Using our minds to get us by and our love like knives

Both sluts and cutters too smart or too stupid to sheath our proverbial weapons

Trying to stay in motion not to let it set in

Unresolved demons are hard to subdue but not harder than banishing thoughts of you

Testing the strength of my integrity, the depth of my commitment, the height of my morality, and the weight of my conscious

Exchanging energy on a spiritual basis, hiding from me that you're knocking up Basics

Hiding something and you did it to well, hiding something you knew you would eventually have to tell

What the fuck was the point?

Almost like you had to make a point to manipulate me too like all the others

Except we don't get to just move on and walk away

We have to suffer daily trying to erase our memory

I know what part of this was me overemphasizing my desire to be free

Trying to protect you from your eagerness to love me

Knowing I was a disaster pure entropy, love, lust, and peace

But once I gave you a piece and you received me, irreversible damage was done

Soul ties were spun, like thread, lead to one another by a notebook inexplicably lost

Never thinking I would meet a fool like me

Intelligence, love and, endless possibility

Curious to see what you would find if I let you explore me

You found a beautiful love I gave to you freely

You gave me the same in return and for that

I have forgave your grievance against me

I will restore our trust and forget your past dishonesty

For your word and opinion could not mean more to me

The warmth of your soul and the value of your insight

A modern black Buddha, your words leading minds from caves to the light

Karen

These white women are not our sisters
Holding their privilege over our heads like
chandeliers
So many shiny things brighten up their room
We look up to see our reflection fragmented into so
many tiny pieces
Reflecting what pride and dignity is left of us
After the system and the ways their men have
taught us gets done with us
A not so pretty picture
The reflection of a damaged and enslaved goddess
Forced to live in a world of Dreams
Where hers are for others consumption
Drank down like the milk for our babies
Our babies they then forced into Slavery
And raped and sold away
There is no truce no treaty
Not with the blood and tears of my ancestors all
around me
Dripping from every tree
The voices call to me and they speak to me kindly,
but they are angry
Filled to completion with fury
We are in no need of white sisterhood or
sympathetic feelings

They will always hate and fear the Africa in me
They sense the magic, the voodoo they never could
do

That natural regality that fueled their jealousy
Hatred for our beauty, they made it their job to
cover up and berate it
According to your rules and standards, we are
Wretched
But our place next to kings, we will reclaim it

Dear White Women,
From your pale bodies and from your blood we will
recreate ourselves
As you created yourself in contrast to us

Violence begets Violence
    Not Benevolence

(Interlude)

I am whole

But I am fragmented having
so many times to gather up
the pieces I could find trying
to remember the pattern

Picking from the options of
who I could still be after those
moments.

Confusion and desperation
the driving force

Dream Being

I have dreams
Let's not let Brother King get the copyright on that
I have dreams
My earliest memories of dream world when I was
nothing but potentiality
I could never quite get the piano down
but I play these keys as the thoughts from that world
come back to me
A past when I was wild and free the words like notes in
my symphony
Trying to bring back that at home feeling
Never typing as fluidly as when the ancestors join me
for a
Meditation on what use to and can still be
For the time it last, I am One with everything and
everyone at peace
Understanding synchronicity in a fleeting moment of
clarity
The feeling of being
That is my dream, to authentically be

Reality

No such thing as coincidence as I see the same
things are always coming to me
My thoughts of magic manifesting in the
conversations of the people around me
Then on TV
Everywhere I am looking
There are innumerable small things who's present
in this reality never eludes and always appears with
the feeling that this is just for me
Left here for me to see
Following the signs the universe leaves me
Always repeating but always changing
Not the things they are always the same
It is me changing
These mementos timeless and never fluctuating
Acting as totems to verify reality from dreams
My reality from the one other's see

Astral Projecting

Always caught between what is and normative
thinking
Trying to use my mind to stop my mind from
spinning
Inner peace hard to conjure while moving
Too much energy used on focusing,
on controlling my breathing
While my body remains in this realm
My mind goes free
Free to travel, meet and convene with entities
previously unseen
Drifting between states of consciousness
But fully conscious
Breaking mental barriers as my notions of reality
collapse
Seeing myself is the first part of the astral journey
I am the subject and Observer
Double Dasein

A Letter to Sensei

We are running in short supply of what it takes to make a great black man

It has been beat and bred out

Hunting dogs right on our trail trying to reach the water to get out

So many bloody bodies, later to see one great black man stand as a God among them a testament to the indestructible matter we are made of

In the firmness of his stance and the kindness of his glance

Energy almost too much to bear as your configuration aligns to the intent of a stronger force

The great black man is aligned to the source and that energy that emanates from him brings you closer to the greatness in yourself as you have been granted access to participate in it

We must all turn our attention to these great black men in hopes that he may once again disseminate to our people the wisdom, patience, and love we lost at the end of whip and noose

Two

I tried so hard to be honest

I have lost sight of truth

I found two

It is said you cannot love two people at once

But I grew these loves

Each in different parts of my garden

Roses and orchids

Two equal forces

Mind and Body

Each influencing me to be countless incarnations
and manifestations of me

A plethora of emotions and desires they illicit from
me

Passive and forcefully drawn to their divinity

With Gods there is no hierarchy

Only what will and always would be

The circle of time repeating

Planting different seeds in me, different tools and
techniques, different ideologies, and beliefs

I have become a planet with two moons

Prism

I was always a light but now I shine through you

My prism taking my light and making something more beautiful

You see the god in me, and I see the God in you

So wrapped up in our legendary love, we forget we are just ordinary people

Just as light passes through a prism your love shines through me and keeps going for eternity

Shining light on all the dark places around me

Giving my world color and clarity

Not Crayola colors but endless possibilities

Giving life a new meaning

Boo'ed up, In my feelings

Your love all encompassing

Rewriting my story and reviving me softly

Putting in more than you take out of me

Healing me of the love deficiency from which I was suffering

Others tried to smother my light, or keep in hidden

But you can never be my past now that you have been my Prism

For God's Sake

You think I hold this love together for me, but I do
it for your sake

A love unconditional in a world that only takes

Takes your time, takes your spirit

And ultimately your life

Hands up don't stop bullets

I am a goddess

Seeing a god defenseless

Naked of his royal gowns and his Crown

Susceptible to any number of perils

Death walking too closely behind them and

A sadness I know too well

A hopelessness that will deceive a God into
forgetting who he is

Lure him off his path to greatness

To shine more love on him than the darkness
around him is the job of the

Goddess

Black King Seen

When I see a Black King it excites something inside
me

Strong in stature and born imbued with his majesty

A descendant like me of ancient dynasties

I feel that power and he feels mine

A coalescence of the ages

As it has happened so many times before and will
happen again one way or the other

On this and alternate planes, in different times by
different names

A Queen will recognize a King

My Time

My two halves always kiss until I let you get in

Where you bang, bend, and distort time and space

You have filled my space, God, but what about my time

The time that got away, the time that was never enough

I made space for you in a time eternal, space folded between ridges of flesh

Yours in mine

Love is the conflation of space and time and I love you even though you are not mine

Everything Love

I loved you like a mother, no I loved you like a slave

Shackled and Subdued

Testing my constraints all the while plotting to escape

But not from you

I will never escape from you

Shrug you off to leave you behind

As if I could ever get a hold of you

Isn't that what I want, to hold you in confession

For you to tell me everything

Everything you know and everything you feel

Everything to be held there entranced by something as
magnificent as me

As my blackness and my black ass

I don't need a hashtag for my magic

You still had your own will after you penetrated my horizon

After we traveled on a path never to be traversed again

A passage between waters to a new destination

How did we arrive at two different places?

Opposing planes separated by vast spaces

Filled up and empty

Sun Low

You always bring me down so low

Down to rest in the airy places among the pebbles

Then beneath them to the dirt

I blow around

I blow here

I blow there

It makes me feel alive

Stimulates a sensor behind my eyes and awakens
the parts unseen

The anti-matter, that which does not matter to you

Who cannot feel its grainy, dampness, and the cold

A cold I could never warm up to

The chill you feel when you are too far from the
Sun to see yourself

Too low to see the light, too far beneath the Sun

Enough Black Blood

Wasted pages writing on tainted white paper.

Black ink bleeding out my own black blood for a thwarted effort

Immersed in all these tainted white things

Would be so pure if not for all the stains left behind

The stains on this soil and every other continent around the world

Feeding on darker flesh and gorging itself on resources

Our flesh culled, taken

Our bodies worked, beaten

Our minds poisoned, deluded

Mental deprived of magic

Bodies deprived of true sensuousness

Using our higher cognitions to navigate a hostile war zone

The descendants of prisoners of a war waged long ago but never formally declared

Declared when the first black body was stolen

When the first plot was laid

Carving out small spaces for ourselves in their world, sidestepping and stepping over the bodies of our fallen

Bleeding Out Black Gods Rise Up

We have taken enough

Tiara Artista is originally from Dallas, Texas growing up she had a love for the arts enriched by her very eclectic Aunt, the late Connie Ann Freeman. Her studies as a creative was continued by her parents enrolling Tiara into performing arts schools where she was an Actor and studied Theatrical Art. Her creativity runs in the family as her Paternal Grandfather, the late Floyd Freeman Senior was a photographer and poet. Today Tiara practices all types of art at Texas State University where she is obtaining her Bachelor of Fine Arts in Studio Art with a Painting Concentration. Tiara's primary media is Oil Paint on canvas and focuses on Black love and intimacy. Tiara Artista uses bright color and images of black couples to showcase the beauty of Black love and its strength. Her work is currently available for purchase at www.tiartista.com and available for viewing on Instagram @tiara.artista . All commission inquiries should be directed to Tiara's email tiara.artista@gmail.com .

www.ingramcontent.com/pod-product-compliance
Lightning Source LLC
Chambersburg PA
CBHW040744250626
47164CB00006BA/169